Your Problem Isn't Your Problem

By

Larry Richman

CENTURY PUBLISHING

SALT LAKE CITY, UTAH

Your Problem Isn't Your Problem

ISBN 978-0-941846-34-9

Portions of this book were developed with the assistance of generative artificial intelligence tools to support idea generation, editing, and organization. All content has been reviewed, curated, and refined by the author to ensure originality, clarity, and quality.

centurypubl.com

info@centurypubl.com

Printed in the United States of America.

Contents

Preface

We live in a world of quick fixes. When something goes wrong, we rush to patch it up—only to find the same issue return. Why? Because we often fix symptoms rather than real problems.

This book will help you dig deeper to see what is really going on. Whether you're facing a personal challenge, a team conflict, or a business setback, the key to lasting change is understanding the root cause.

In this book, you'll find real-life examples, simple tools, and a clear way to solve problems better. When you learn to ask the right questions, you'll find better answers.

CHAPTER 1

The Problem with Problems

Why we often solve the wrong thing—and what it costs us.

We all face problems. Some are small—like a leaky faucet. Others are big—like a failing business or a broken relationship. But no matter the size, we often make the same mistake: we try to fix what we see on the surface, not what's really going on.

The Quick Fix Trap

Imagine your car starts making a strange noise. You turn up the radio, so you don't hear it. Problem solved, right?

Of course not. You've only masked the symptoms. The real issue—maybe a loose belt or worn brakes—is still there. And it's getting worse.

We do the same thing at home and at work. A team misses deadlines, so we add more meetings. A child acts out, so we take away screen time. A product isn't selling, so we lower the price. These are quick fixes. They might help for a moment, but they don't solve the real problem.

A Real-Life Example: The Call Center

A large company had a problem: customer satisfaction scores were dropping. The solution seemed obvious—train the call center staff to be more polite. So, they rolled out a new training program, complete with scripts and smiley-face stickers.

But the scores didn't improve.

Eventually, someone asked a deeper question: *Why are customers unhappy in the first place?*

After some digging, they discovered that the real issue wasn't the tone of the calls—it was the wait time. Customers were frustrated before they even spoke to anyone. The root cause wasn't rudeness. It was understaffing.

Once they hired more agents and improved the call routing system, satisfaction scores went up—without any more smiley-face stickers.

Why We Miss the Real Problem

There are a few reasons we tend to treat symptoms instead of causes:

- **It's faster.** Digging deeper takes time, and we're often in a hurry.
- **It's easier.** Surface problems are more visible and feel more manageable.
- **It feels productive.** Doing *something*—even if it's the wrong thing—feels better than doing nothing.

But solving the wrong problem is like putting a bandage on a broken bone. It might cover the wound, but it won't help you heal.

The Cost of Solving the Wrong Problem

When we don't address the root cause, problems come back—sometimes bigger than before. We waste time, money, and energy. We frustrate ourselves and others. And we miss opportunities to make real progress.

This book is about changing that.

It's about learning to pause, look deeper, and ask better questions. It's about finding the real problem—so you can solve it once and for all.

Reflection

What problems in my life am I trying to solve with a quick fix?

Have I recently addressed a symptom instead of the real problem?

What issue keeps coming back despite my efforts to fix it?

CHAPTER 2

Symptoms vs. Causes

How to tell the difference and why it matters.

When something goes wrong, our first instinct is to fix what we see. But what we see is often just the surface—the symptom. The real problem lies underneath.

The Iceberg Principle

Think of a problem like an iceberg. The part above the water is what's visible: missed deadlines, poor sales, low morale. But the bulk of the iceberg—the root cause—is hidden beneath the surface. If we only chip away at what we can see, we're not really solving anything.

A Story: The Slipping Grades

Consider a high school student named Maya. Her grades suddenly drop, and her teachers assume she's not studying. They assign more homework and call her parents.

But Maya's problem isn't laziness. Her family recently moved, and she's struggling to adjust. She misses her old friends. She feels lost. The real issue is emotional, not academic.

Once her counselor helps her talk through the transition, her grades begin to recover—without extra homework.

This is the difference between treating a symptom and addressing a cause.

How to Spot a Symptom

Symptoms are:

- **Immediate**: They show up quickly.
- **Visible**: Easy to notice and describe.
- **Emotional**: They often trigger frustration, fear, or urgency.

Examples:

- A team misses a deadline.
- A customer leaves a bad review.
- A partner stops communicating.

These are signs that something is wrong—but not explanations of *why* it's wrong.

How to Find the Cause

Causes are:

- **Hidden**: They require digging.
- **Systemic**: Often part of a larger pattern.
- **Rooted in behavior, structure, or belief.**

To find them, ask:

- What's really going on here?
- Has this happened before?
- What changed recently?
- What assumptions am I making?

The 5 Whys Technique

One simple tool is the "5 Whys." You ask "why?" five times to peel back the layers.

Example problem: The report was late.

1. Why? The team didn't finish on time.

2. Why? They were waiting for the data.
3. Why? The data team was behind.
4. Why? They had too many requests.
5. Why? There's no system to prioritize tasks.

Now you're getting somewhere. The real issue isn't the report—it's poor workflow management.

Why This Matters

When we treat symptoms:

- Problems return.
- We waste time and energy.
- We frustrate ourselves and others.

When we find causes:

- We solve problems for good.
- We build trust and clarity.
- We grow stronger systems and relationships.

Key Takeaway

Symptoms are signals. Causes are the story behind the signal. If you want real change, stop reacting to what's visible and start investigating what's hidden.

Reflection

What is a current problem I'm facing? Is it a symptom or a cause?

____

____

____

____

____

Have I asked "why" enough times to find the real issue?

____

____

____

____

____

What assumptions am I making about this problem?

____

____

____

____

____

CHAPTER 3

The Power of the Pause

Slowing down to ask better questions.

In a fast-paced world, pausing feels counterintuitive. We're taught to act quickly, respond immediately, and keep moving. But when it comes to solving problems, speed can be the enemy of insight.

Why We Rush

We rush because:

- We feel pressure to fix things fast.
- We want to look competent.
- We're uncomfortable with uncertainty.

But rushing often leads to shallow solutions. We treat what's obvious, not what's important.

A Story: The Broken Team

A manager named Carlos noticed his team was disengaged. Meetings were quiet. Deadlines were missed. He assumed the problem was motivation, so he scheduled a pep talk and offered bonuses.

Nothing changed.

Instead of pushing harder, Carlos paused. He asked his team what was going on. He listened. He learned that the real issue was confusion—roles weren't clear, and expectations kept shifting.

Once he clarified responsibilities and gave the team space to speak up, things improved. The pause made all the difference.

What Pausing Looks Like

Pausing isn't passive. It's intentional.

It means:

- Asking questions before offering answers.
- Observing patterns before jumping to conclusions.
- Reflecting on your own assumptions.

It's the moment between reaction and response.

Tools for Pausing

Here are a few ways to build the habit:

- **Ask, Don't Assume.** Instead of "I know what's wrong," try "What might be going on here?"
- **Journal the Problem.** Write down what you see, what you feel, and what you suspect. Often, clarity comes through writing.
- **Talk It Out.** Share the issue with someone outside the situation. A fresh perspective can reveal blind spots.
- **Wait 24 Hours.** If possible, give yourself a day before acting. Urgency often fades, and insight grows.

The Benefits of Pausing

When you pause:

- You make space for deeper thinking.
- You reduce emotional reactivity.
- You increase the chance of solving the *right* problem.

Pausing isn't weakness. It's wisdom.

Key Takeaway

The pause is where clarity lives. Before you fix, listen. Before you act, reflect. The best solutions often come after the quiet moment when you stop and ask, "What's really going on here?"

Reflection

When was the last time I paused before reacting to a problem?

What did I learn the last time I reflected before acting?

What would happen if I paused longer before solving this issue?

CHAPTER 4

Patterns, Not Just Events

How recurring issues reveal deeper truths.

Most of us treat problems as isolated events. Something goes wrong, we fix it and move on. But what if that problem isn't a one-time thing? What if it's part of a pattern?

The Power of Patterns

Patterns are repeated behaviors, outcomes, or dynamics. They're the trail left behind by deeper causes. If you can spot the pattern, you can trace it back to the root.

A Story: The Late Deliveries

A small business owner named Jenna kept running into the same issue: her orders were late. At first, she blamed the shipping company. Then she blamed her staff. She even considered switching suppliers.

But after stepping back, she noticed a pattern. The delays always happened at the end of the month. Why?

She realized her team was overwhelmed with end-of-month reporting, which pulled them away from packing and shipping. The real issue wasn't the shipping—it was poor scheduling.

Once she adjusted the workflow, the delays stopped.

Why We Miss Patterns

We're wired to focus on the immediate:

- What just happened?
- Who's responsible?
- How do I fix it now?

But this short-term thinking blinds us to long-term trends. We treat each problem like it's new, when it's really part of a bigger picture.

How to Spot a Pattern

Ask yourself:

- Has this happened before?
- When does it usually happen?
- Who is usually involved?
- What else is going on at the same time?

Look for:

- **Timing** (for example, always at the end of the quarter)
- **People** (for example, same team or customer)
- **Conditions** (for example, high stress, low resources)

Patterns Reveal Systems

Most problems don't exist in isolation. They're part of a system—how people, processes, and expectations interact. Patterns help you see the system, not just the symptom.

When you recognize the system, you can change it.

A Simple Exercise: The Pattern Log

Start a "pattern log." Every time a problem occurs, jot down:

- What happened
- When it happened
- Who was involved
- What else was happening

After a few entries, you'll start to see connections. Those connections are clues.

Key Takeaway

Don't just fix the event. Find the pattern. Patterns point to systems, and systems point to causes. When you solve the system, you solve the problem—for good.

Reflection

What recurring challenges am I facing?

____

____

____

____

____

What patterns do I see in my work, relationships, or habits?

____

____

____

____

____

What system might be contributing to this pattern?

____

____

____

____

____

CHAPTER 5

Assumptions Are Invisible Walls

Challenging what you think you know.

We all make assumptions. They help us move through life without overthinking every detail. But when it comes to solving problems, assumptions can be dangerous. They act like invisible walls—limiting what we see, what we ask, and what we try.

What Are Assumptions?

Assumptions are beliefs we accept without proof. They're shortcuts our brains take to make sense of the world. Some are helpful. But others keep us stuck.

We assume:

- We know what the problem is.
- We know what others are thinking.
- We know what will or won't work.

These assumptions shape our decisions—and sometimes lead us in the wrong direction.

A Story: The Failing Campaign

A nonprofit launched a fundraising campaign that flopped. The team assumed the problem was the message—it wasn't emotional enough. So, they rewrote it, added more stories, and tried again.

Still no traction.

Eventually, someone asked: What if the problem isn't the message?

They discovered their emails were going to spam folders. The real issue wasn't emotional appeal—it was technical. Their assumption had blinded them to the actual cause.

Once they fixed the email settings, donations started coming in.

How Assumptions Limit Us

Assumptions:

- Narrow our focus.
- Block new ideas.
- Prevent us from asking better questions.

They're especially dangerous when they're unconscious—when we don't even realize we're making them.

How to Challenge Assumptions

Start by noticing them. Ask:

- What am I assuming here?
- Is that actually true?
- What else could be going on?

Try flipping the assumption:

- If you assume someone is lazy, ask: What if they're overwhelmed?
- If you assume a system is broken, ask: What if it's being misused?

A Simple Tool: The Assumption Audit

Write down your assumptions about a problem. Then, for each one, ask:

- What evidence supports this?
- What evidence contradicts it?
- What would happen if this assumption is wrong?

This exercise can reveal blind spots—and open new paths forward.

Key Takeaway

Assumptions are invisible walls. They limit your thinking and block real solutions. When you learn to spot and challenge them, you break through those walls—and discover what's possible.

Reflection

What assumptions might I be making that limit my thinking?

What would I try if I believed my current assumption was wrong?

Who could help me challenge my assumptions?

CHAPTER 6

The Root Cause Mindset

Cultivating curiosity, humility, and clarity.

Solving problems at the root isn't just a technique—it's a mindset. It's a way of thinking that values depth over speed, clarity over certainty, and curiosity over control.

What Is a Root Cause Mindset?

It's the habit of asking:

- What's really going on here?
- What's beneath the surface?
- What am I missing?

It's the willingness to sit with uncertainty, to explore uncomfortable truths, and to keep digging even when the first answer feels "good enough."

A Story: The Burned-Out Leader

Marcus was a department head in a growing company. He was exhausted, overwhelmed, and ready to quit. He assumed the problem was the workload—too many meetings, too many emails.

So, he tried time management hacks. He blocked off his mornings. He unsubscribed from newsletters. He even hired an assistant.

Nothing worked.

Then a mentor asked him, *"Why do you say yes to everything?"*

That question hit hard. Marcus realized the real issue wasn't his calendar—it was his fear of disappointing others. He believed that saying "no" made him look weak or unhelpful.

Once he addressed that belief, everything changed. He started setting boundaries. His energy returned. His team respected him more.

The root cause wasn't time—it was identity.

Three Traits of the Root Cause Mindset

- **Curiosity.** You don't assume you know the answer. You ask questions. You explore. You wonder.
- **Humility.** You accept that you might be wrong. You're open to feedback. You're willing to change your mind.
- **Patience.** You resist the urge to fix things fast. You give yourself time to understand before you act.

How to Cultivate the Mindset

- **Start with "Why?"** Not just once—ask it multiple times. Go deeper.
- **Look inward first.** Before blaming others or external factors, ask: *What part of this do I own?*
- **Be okay with not knowing.** Sometimes the root cause isn't obvious. That's okay. Stay with the question.
- **Celebrate insight, not just action.** Progress isn't just doing something—it's understanding something new.

Key Takeaway

The root cause mindset is about how you think, not just what you do. It's a way of approaching problems with curiosity, humility, and patience—so you can solve them at the source, not just on the surface.

Reflection

How can I better approach problems with curiosity and humility?

What uncomfortable truth might I be avoiding?

What would a root-cause mindset look like in this situation?

CHAPTER 7

Tools for Digging Deeper

Simple methods to uncover what's really going on.

Understanding the root cause of a problem isn't just about mindset—it's also about method. In this chapter, we'll explore simple, practical tools that help you dig beneath the surface and uncover what's really going on.

Even with the right mindset, it's easy to get stuck. Emotions, assumptions, and complexity can cloud our thinking. Tools give us structure. They help us slow down, ask better questions, and stay focused on the deeper issue.

Tool #1: The Five Whys

This classic technique helps you peel back the layers of a problem by asking "why?" repeatedly.

Example problem: The project was late.

- Why? The team missed the deadline.
- Why? They didn't have the data.
- Why? The data wasn't ready.
- Why? The analyst was overloaded.
- Why? There's no backup plan for high-demand periods.

Now you're at a root cause: lack of resource planning.

Tip: Don't stop at the first "why." Keep going until you hit something systemic.

Tool #2: The Problem Tree

Draw a tree:

- The **leaves** are symptoms.
- The **branches** are contributing factors.
- The **roots** are the underlying causes.

This visual tool helps you see how everything connects—and where to focus your energy.

Tool #3: The "What Else?" Question

When you think you've found the cause, ask:

- What else could be contributing?
- What else might I be missing?
- What else has changed recently?

This keeps your thinking open and prevents tunnel vision.

Tool #4: Stakeholder Interviews

Talk to people involved in or affected by the problem. Ask:

- What do you think is causing this?
- When did you first notice it?
- What's been tried already?

You'll often uncover insights you wouldn't find on your own.

Tool #5: Timeline Mapping

Lay out the events leading up to the problem. Look for:

- Triggers or turning points
- Delays or breakdowns
- Repeated patterns

This helps you understand the context and sequence of events.

Tool #6: Assumption Surfacing

List your assumptions about the problem. Then challenge each one:

- Is this always true?
- What if it's not?
- What would I do differently if this assumption were false?

This tool pairs well with Chapter 5.

Tool #7: Root Cause Brainstorming

Gather a small group and ask: *What could be causing this?*

Encourage wild ideas. Don't judge. Then group the ideas into themes and explore the most promising ones.

Key Takeaway

Tools don't solve problems for you—but they help you think more clearly. Use them to slow down, dig deeper, and stay focused on what really matters.

Reflection

How could I use tools like the Five Whys or Problem Tree on my current problem?

____

____

____

____

____

What new questions could help me dig deeper?

____

____

____

____

____

Who else should I talk to about this problem?

____

____

____

____

____

CHAPTER 8

Solving the Right Problem

How to take actions that actually work.

You've learned how to pause, question assumptions, spot patterns, and dig deeper. Now it's time to bring it all together—to solve the *right* problem.

Why This Chapter Matters

Solving the right problem means your effort leads to real change. It means you stop spinning your wheels and start moving forward. It's the difference between treating a symptom and creating a solution that lasts.

A Story: The Stuck Startup

A startup was struggling to grow. The founders thought the problem was marketing—they weren't getting enough leads. So, they hired a new agency, spent more on ads, and redesigned their website.

Still no growth.

Eventually, they talked to their customers and discovered the real issue: the product didn't solve a big enough problem. It was "nice to have," not "need to have."

They went back to the drawing board, refined their offering, and focused on a more urgent customer pain point. Growth followed.

They had been trying to solve the wrong problem. Once they found the right one, everything changed.

How to Know You've Found the Right Problem

Ask yourself:

- Does solving this make other problems easier or irrelevant?
- Is this issue recurring, or is it a one-time event?
- Have past solutions failed because they didn't address this?

The right problem is usually:

- **Deeper** than it first appears
- **Connected** to other issues
- **Actionable**—you can do something about it

From Insight to Action

Once you've identified the root cause, take action—but do it wisely.

- **Start Small.** Test your solution on a small scale. See what works. Adjust.
- **Measure What Matters.** Track the impact of your solution. Are the symptoms improving? Are new issues emerging?
- **Stay Curious.** Even after you act, keep asking questions. Root causes can shift. New patterns can emerge.

A Final Tool: The Problem Statement

Write a clear, concise statement of the problem you're solving. Include:

- What's happening.
- Why it matters.
- What's causing it.

Example:

"Our team misses deadlines because roles are unclear and priorities shift weekly, leading to confusion and rework."

This keeps everyone focused on the real issue—not just the noise around it.

Key Takeaway

Solving the right problem is the goal of everything you've learned. It's not about fixing fast—it's about fixing well. When you solve the right problem, you create real, lasting change.

Reflection

Am I confident that I've identified the right problem?

Will solving this issue address deeper or recurring problems?

Write a clear, concise statement of the problem I need to solve.

CONCLUSION

From Symptom to Root Cause

We live in a world that rewards speed, celebrates quick fixes, and often overlooks the deeper story. But real progress—lasting, meaningful change—comes when we slow down and look beneath the surface.

Throughout this book, you've explored the difference between symptoms and causes. You've learned to pause, to question, to notice patterns, and to challenge assumptions. You've practiced thinking like a root cause detective—curious, humble, and patient.

This isn't just a method. It's a mindset. And it's one you can carry into every part of your life.

- When a relationship feels strained, ask what's really going on.
- When a project stalls, look beyond the obvious.
- When you feel stuck, dig deeper—not just into the problem, but into yourself.

The tools you've learned are simple, but powerful. Use them. Share them. Refine them. And most of all, trust that the time you spend understanding the real problem is never wasted.

Because when you solve the right problem, you don't just fix what's broken, you build something better.

Other Books in This Series

Your Problem Isn't Your Problem. Solve the right problem. Solve the root cause rather than treat symptoms.

> *What if the problem you're trying to solve isn't the real problem? Learn to distinguish between symptoms and causes. Challenge assumptions that limit your thinking. Take action that solves the root cause of problems.*

My Problem Isn't Your Problem. Take responsibility for your problems. Don't blame, deflect, or expect others to fix your problems

> *Learn how to replace blame with responsibility, let go of excuses, and take real action at work, at home, and in your relationships. Shift from a victim mindset to one of leadership and agency.*

Your Problem Isn't My Problem. Set healthy boundaries. Stop rescuing others and allow them to solve their own problems.

> *Understand when to help others and when to step back. Learn about setting boundaries, detaching emotionally from others' outcomes, and supporting others without enabling bad behavior.*

About the Author

Larry Richman is a writer, speaker, and personal development coach known for his clear, practical approach to solving real-life challenges. With decades of experience helping individuals and organizations grow, he specializes in cutting through confusion to get to the heart of what really matters. His writing is refreshingly direct, relatable, and filled with tools you can use today to create lasting change.

www.ingramcontent.com/pod-product-compliance
Lightning Source LLC
LaVergne TN
LVHW010548100826
845148LV00013B/2656

* 9 7 8 0 9 4 1 8 4 6 3 4 9 *